Classy as Fuck Cocktails

60+ Damn Good Recipes for All Occasions

By Calligraphuck

CHRONICLE BOOKS
SAN FRANCISCO

Contents

Introduction

Fuck yeah—it's time for a drink! A well-mixed cocktail is a truly versatile accessory. Special occasion? This deserves a toast! Stressful week? Chill out with a stiff drink. Staying booze-free right now? You deserve something grown-up and delicious, too.

If you're going to have a drink, why not make it a damn fine one? Ordering a cocktail from a pro is a safe bet for a great tipple, but there's a unique satisfaction to be earned from making something with your own hands.

This book will cover a diversity of mixed drinks to fit nearly any occasion. The classics are here, some with a history going back centuries, as well as new classics from the craft cocktail revival of the last few decades. Also there are dozens of variations, easy substitutions, and cheeky twists to help you find your long-lost soul mate in a glass.

If you've never mixed a drink before, but always wanted to, we hope this book is the kick in the ass you need. If you know your way around a home bar already, we hope you'll uncover something new and inspiring. Now go make a damn delicious cocktail!

Cheers to good fucking health,

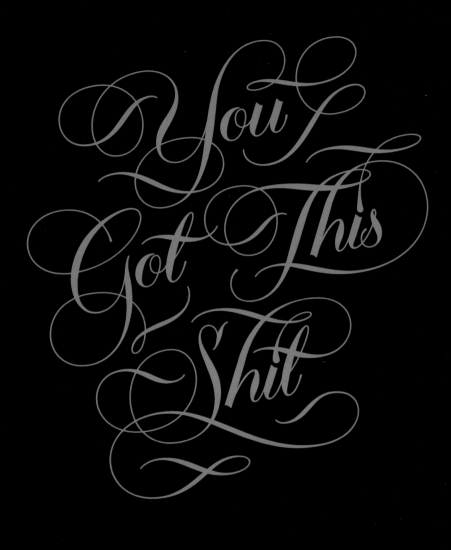

Home Bar Basics

Whether it's photography, music, or cycling, a fun and addictive part of any hobby is obsessing over gear. Just don't let a lack of equipment become an excuse to avoid getting your hands dirty and giving it a try. That's why we've suggested a substitute you can use in a pinch if you're missing a tool or away from your home bar. Use whatever you have for now and make a fucking drink!

Hardware

Cocktail Shaker

The two most common styles of shakers are the Cobbler and Boston Shaker. The Cobbler consists of three metal pieces: the main body, a strainer, and a lid. The Boston Shaker comprises a metal tin and a glass cup that interlock.

Alternative: Lidded jar or wide-mouth bottle.

Jigger

As the measuring cup is to baking, the jigger is to cocktails. The double-sided conical design is most common, although an angled measuring cup is more user-friendly, if maybe slightly less sexy.

Alternative: A shot glass can hold 1 to 2 oz [30 to 60 ml], so it can be used as an emergency measure.

Mixing Glass

Specially designed for mixing drinks, a mixing (or stirring) glass has straight sides, a heavy base, and a spout.

Alternative: Pint glass or glass jar.

Strainer

The julep strainer is an oversized perforated spoon, used for mixed drinks. The Hawthorne features a coiled spring and fits snugly inside a Boston Shaker. In addition, a fine-mesh strainer is used for "double straining."

Alternative: Sieve, slotted spoon, or tea strainer.

Barspoon

A long-handled spoon with a spiral or rounded stem for easy stirring.

Alternative: Chopstick or butter knife. For floating use the back of a teaspoon.

Additional Tools

Other handy tools include a citrus squeezer—lever or reamer style (in a pinch use your hands, just be careful of the seeds)—and a vegetable peeler for making citrus twists. A wooden muddler is useful for some drinks, but you can always use the handle of a wooden spoon.

Glassware

A well-made drink can be served in a cardboard cup, a coffee mug, or an old fuckin' boot, and it will still taste delicious. That said, part of the fun is in the presentation. There are many styles of glassware, but if you're starting out, try to pick up a few in the three main styles:

1   Served Up

Cocktail glass, aka coupe (bowl-shaped) or martini (v-shaped) glass. Stemmed glassware for serving mixed drinks without ice. Holds 6 to 8 oz [180 to 240 ml].

2   Served on the Rocks

Rocks glass, aka old fashioned glass. A stout glass for serving strong drinks usually with ice (without ice would be served "neat"). Standard size holds 6 to 8 oz [180 to 240 ml]; double holds 12 to 15 oz [360 to 450 ml].

3   Served Long

Highball or Collins glass. Tall glasses for serving drinks topped with a carbonated mixer or other lighter drinks. Holds 10 to 16 oz [300 to 480 ml].

Most of the drinks in this book will call for one of these three styles. Some recipes will suggest a more obscure glass like a hurricane glass or a mule cup, but feel free to substitute whatever you have that will do the job.

Techniques

Chilling

Warm surfaces are the enemy of ice, so it's imperative for every item your drink touches to be as cold as possible. Place your glassware in the fridge 15 minutes ahead, or add ice water for a couple of minutes and discard before serving.

Stirring

Drinks that contain only spirits are usually stirred. The goal is to chill and gently dilute. Fill your chilled mixing glass with the ingredients, then add as much ice as you can fit without spilling over. Briskly but gently stir in a circular motion with a barspoon for about 30 seconds.

Shaking

Drinks that contain citrus, eggs, dairy, or other cloudy ingredients are usually shaken. Add your ingredients with a generous helping of ice to the shaker base (or glass with a Boston Shaker). Cap with the top (or add the shaking tin, at a slight angle, and tap into place). Hold with both hands, with your dominant hand on the top. Shake vigorously as all hell in an up-and-down motion for about 15 seconds, or until the shaker is frosty. Uncap (or strike the shaking tin with your palm to dislodge). Strain through the built-in strainer (or a Hawthorne strainer).

Dry Shaking

Shaking without ice is an additional step for drinks with egg whites for an extra-foamy finish. Dry shake for 30 seconds to 1 minute. If using a Boston Shaker, add the shaking tin straight-on, not at an angle, to avoid leakage.

Rolling

Use this technique when chilling and dilution are needed, but without the aeration of shaking. It requires a pair of vessels, either two large cups or one large cup, plus a shaking tin. Add the ingredients with ice to one of the two vessels, being careful not to overfill (aim for two-thirds full). Pour from one vessel to the other, back and forth, two or three times. Strain or pour into the serving glass.

Floating

Some drinks call for distinct layering by floating different ingredients on top of the previous. The key is to pour slowly over the back of a spoon. Think of it as the difference between the gentle sprinkle of water from a shower versus the hard jet of water from a garden hose. The float should be shower-like.

Salting a Glass Rim

Rub a wedge of either lime or lemon around the rim of the glass, then turn upside down onto a saucer with salt. Avoid fine-grain salt like table salt; stick with kosher or lightly crushed flaky sea salt.

Spirits

Brandy

Cognac (France) is the most famous region for brandy making, but since you're mixing it, don't go for the most expensive stuff—look for a well-priced VSOP (Very Superior Old Pale). Brandy can be made with any fruit, but unless otherwise specified, our recipes call for brandy made from grapes.

Gin

A classic London dry gin is the most called for in cocktails. Many artisan gins are now available, each with a different bouquet of botanicals, less juniper-forward than the classic brands. Old Tom-style gin is sweeter and will give a different twist to a gin and tonic and other long drinks.

Rum

Start with a bottle of white (unaged) rum and a bottle of dark (aged) rum. Gold rum is somewhere between. Spiced dark rum can be killer in a Dark 'n' Stormy but is less versatile for cocktail making, unless you're looking to dive deep into tiki-land.

Tequila and Mezcal

Start with a bottle of blanco, aka silver tequila, made with 100 percent blue agave. Reposado and añejo tequila are aged in wood, are more expensive, and should be used judiciously. Mezcal is a distilled spirit made from roasted agave that's become increasingly popular in cocktails. Look for an affordable bottle made with *espadín* agave.

Vodka

Vodka should taste neutral. Pick value over fancy marketing.

Whiskey

Start with a decent bottle of bourbon (sweet, fuller body) or rye (spicy, drier), then a blended Scotch. Irish, Canadian, and Japanese whiskies make great further additions if you find it's the spirit that compels you most. A smoky peated (Islay) single-malt Scotch will come in handy for a few recipes.

Other Ingredients

Amaro

Amari are a subset of bitter Italian liqueurs. Campari is the most famous and frequently called for, along with Aperol. Others can be more challenging (see page 120 for more details).

Aromatic Bitters

Angostura is a must-have for any home bar. After Angostura, look for Peychaud's or orange bitters. Beyond the basics, there is a huge variety of flavored bitters available from grapefruit to chocolate.

Dry Sparkling Wine

Champagne (France) has the name recognition, but the more budget-conscious Cava (Spain) and Prosecco (Italy) will shine equally in any cocktail that calls for sparkling wine.

Liqueur

Orange liqueur is a very useful ingredient: Triple Sec (Cointreau is one brand), orange curaçao, or Grand Marnier all work. Additional liqueurs are nice to have, but invest in flavors you really enjoy.

Vermouth

Both sweet and dry vermouth are called for in different recipes. Vermouth, like all wine, will spoil. Keep it in the fridge for up to a month after opening.

Ice

As a rule of thumb, when serving, use the biggest and clearest ice you can get your hands on. Your drink will dilute more slowly and will look sexy as hell.

Ice is probably the deepest rabbit hole you can fall into in the world of cocktails. Aficionados obsess about clarity and surface area as though it were unobtainium and not frozen H_2O. Don't get hung up on it; use the ice cubes from the tray in your freezer or from the supermarket to start with. You can always go down the rabbit hole later.

For clear ice, use boiled (then cooled) or distilled water.

Punch Ice

Fill a loaf pan, plastic food storage container, or similar vessel with water and freeze overnight. Run the container under hot water to loosen.

To kick things up a fucking level, layer fruit inside your punch ice. Add fruit or strips of lemon zest to the bottom of your container, then ice cubes to keep them from floating to the top. Top with water and freeze as above.

Eggs, most frequently egg whites, add a rich foam and texture when used in cocktails. Always use fresh eggs. Despite the extremely low risk of salmonella, if it's a concern, you can always use pasteurized eggs or pasteurized liquid egg whites. Keep chilled until needed.

Egg White Alternatives

If egg allergies are a concern, or you're looking for a plant-based alternative, you may have heard of aquafaba from the world of vegan baking. Sadly, it's not effective in cocktails. Fortunately, a number of companies have made tinctures from soapbark (*Quillaja saponaria*) that do a great job of foaming with minimum impact on flavor. Brands include Fee Brothers Fee Foam, Addiction Mixology InstaFoam, and Ms. Better's Bitters Miraculous Foamer.

Simple Syrups

At its heart, simple syrup is just sugar water. It's used in cocktails instead of sugar to prevent any undissolved granules in your drink. It's super fucking easy to prepare, and making variations is a cinch. White sugar is standard, but demerara or turbinado sugar will give a nice caramel note.

Simple Syrup
(1:1 sugar to water)

1 cup [240 ml] water

1 cup + 3 Tbsp [245 g] sugar

Spiced Variations

Habañero:
Add 4 sliced habañero chiles, with seeds

Makrut lime leaf:
Add 10 leaves, roughly chopped

Star anise:
Add 10 anise pods, crushed

Rich Simple Syrup
(2:1 sugar to water)

1 cup [240 ml] water

2 cups [400 g] sugar

Rich Honey Syrup
(2:1 honey to water)

1 cup [240 ml] water

2 cups [680 g] honey

Honey-Ginger Syrup

1 cup [240 ml] water

1 cup [340 g] honey

1 large ginger root, peeled and sliced

Method

Boil the water in a microwave or in a saucepan. Add the boiling liquid to a heatproof bowl with the remaining ingredients. Mix completely until the sugar or honey is completely dissolved.

If adding flavoring ingredients that will not dissolve, let stand for 30 minutes before straining through a fine-mesh sieve and discarding the solids.

Store in a clean, airtight container in the fridge for up to 3 weeks. Or to extend shelf life, add ⅔ oz [20 ml] vodka to keep up to 3 months.

Other Syrups

For the following syrups, which do not use water as a base, follow the same method, but do not boil the liquid. Heat slowly and gently on the stove, or microwave room-temperature juice or milk for 20 seconds at a time, until warm enough to dissolve the sugar.

Grenadine

1 cup [240 ml] unsweetened pomegranate juice

1 cup [200 g] sugar

1 oz [30 ml] pomegranate molasses (optional)

Orgeat

1 cup [240 ml] unsweetened almond milk

½ cup plus 1½ Tbsp [120 g] sugar

¼ tsp almond extract

¼ tsp orange blossom or rose water

Shrubs

Shrubs are acidic fruit syrups, usually made with vinegar. They're fruity, sweet, and tart with a wonderful depth of flavor. You do need to plan ahead a little, as the longer you can leave them to sit, the better the flavors will meld.

Making shrubs predates refrigeration and is used to preserve fruit, so it's a great way to reduce waste. Use fruit that's overripe, bruised, or wonky looking—it'll still taste fan-fucking-tastic! The following recipe is an example, but experiment for yourself: Just use roughly equal parts by weight of fruit, sugar and vinegar, then balance to taste.

Pear and Fig Shrub

3 small soft ripe pears, quartered

3 plump fresh figs, quartered

1 cup [200 g] brown sugar

½ tsp vanilla bean paste or vanilla extract

½ tsp ground cardamom

¼ tsp black pepper, cracked

7 oz [210 ml] apple cider vinegar or rice wine vinegar

Add all the ingredients to a nonreactive container. Muddle well. Cover with plastic wrap and leave in a cool, dark spot for 2 to 4 days (the longer the better). Stir once a day. Once matured, strain through a nonreactive mesh strainer, pushing down on the fruit pulp for maximum extraction. Transfer to a clean bottle and store sealed in the fridge for up to 2 months.

Tea-Infused Spirits

Combine tea and clear spirit in a glass jar or bottle. Use three tea bags or roughly 4 Tbsp [8 g] loose leaf tea per standard bottle of spirits. Cap and roll the jar or bottle gently to saturate tea.

Let steep for 2 hours at room temperature when using black tea; softer teas like white tea may require up to twice as long to infuse. Pour through a mesh strainer into a clean container. Avoid pressing down on the tea leaves in the strainer to increase yield—this will introduce unwanted bitterness to the infusion.

Substitutions

Cream of Coconut

Cream of coconut is a sweetened coconut product, Coco López being the original brand from Puerto Rico. If it's hard to find or overpriced in your area, try this substitution: Refrigerate a can of full-fat coconut milk overnight to allow the water and cream to separate. Once chilled, open from the bottom and discard (or reserve and drink) the coconut water. Combine two parts coconut cream with one part orgeat syrup or rich simple syrup (pages 18 and 19).

Pimm's No. 1

Pimm's is ubiquitous across Britain during summer, but it can be difficult to source in other countries. Here's a quick and dirty alternative: Replace Pimm's with equal parts gin, sweet vermouth, and Triple Sec. Compared to the original, it's more bitter and citrus-forward, but some may consider that a bonus.

Top Tips

As you get going, keep in mind a few basic principles, and you'll be fucking golden:

1. Chill your glass before serving.

2. When batching, chill your bottles.

3. Stir if it's booze only; shake if ingredients include juice, eggs, or dairy.

4. Use the freshest juice possible.

5. Use the biggest, clearest ice possible.

6. Add your carbonated ingredients just before serving to avoid losing bubbles.

7. If a top-off is called for, start with a little, taste, then adjust. You can always dilute further, but you can't undilute.

8. Always taste your drink. Add sugar or citrus to balance sweetness and acidity.

9. Enjoy your-damn-self!

Fuck Yeah, Celebrate!

Delightful drinks for high-spirited occasions

The philosopher Socrates said that worthless people live only to eat and drink; people of worth eat and drink only to live. With an attitude like that, no wonder the last drink he was offered was laced with poison. What a fucking buzzkill!

Food and drink don't merely sustain life—they're the colors with which we paint our most cherished memories. Celebrations with dear friends and family. A sparkling toast to a new milestone or achievement. The nights that stretch into the early morning with too much good drink and equally great company! The plates and glasses we lingered over on the night we met the love of our life. Those are the things that make life worth living.

The glass raised is the hallmark of communal celebration across the world. So if it's worth raising, why not fill it with something damn delicious? Regardless of the season, setting, or occasion, hopefully this chapter helps you find the libation fit for your celebration!

Margarita

The quintessential good-time drink. It's hard to resist the charms of a classic marg. Plus, once you have it down, there are a myriad of variations to enjoy.

Lime wedge

Kosher salt or flaky sea salt

2 oz [60 ml] tequila

½ oz [15 ml] Triple Sec

1 oz [30 ml] fresh lime juice

Lime wedge, for garnish

Method

Rim a chilled margarita glass with salt and set aside (see page 13 and Note below). In an ice-filled cocktail shaker, combine the tequila, Triple Sec, and lime juice. Shake. Strain into the salt-rimmed glass. Garnish with the lime wedge.

NOTES & VARIATIONS

Salt rims look great, but drink messy. If you'd rather avoid the cleanup, skip the rim, and add a pinch of salt directly to the shaker instead.

Bloody Mezcal Margarita: Replace the tequila with mezcal and add 1 oz [30 ml] blood orange juice to the mix.

Caipirinha

Name any country that knows how to have a better time than Brazil. Carnival is so huge, the country basically takes the month off to party and drink Caipirinhas! Clearly, they're doing something the fuck right.

Method

In a sturdy double rocks glass, muddle together the lime wedges and sugar. Add ice, ⅔ oz [20 ml] chilled water, and cachaça.

½ lime, sliced into wedges

2 tsp superfine sugar

2 oz [60 ml] cachaça

NOTES & VARIATIONS

Adding fresh fruit is an easy and mouthwatering way to make Caipirinha variations. Try tropical fruits such as mango, guava, pineapple, or kiwi. Simply add to the muddle with the lime wedges and sugar.

Sakerinha: Brazil is home to the world's largest Japanese diaspora, so replacing cachaça with sake was bound to happen. Awesome with sushi.

Mojito

The smooth, chill appeal and easy drinkability of the Mojito is hard to beat. It's the perfect start to a long weekend, a liquid embodiment of feeling refreshed and restored. And if you have one too many, you can always sleep it off tomorrow.

6 large mint leaves

¾ oz [22 ml] simple syrup (page 18)

¾ oz [22 ml] fresh lime juice

2 oz [60 ml] white rum

Soda water, to top up

Mint sprig, for garnish

Straw, to serve

Method

In the bottom of a cocktail shaker, muddle the mint leaves. Add the simple syrup, lime juice, and rum. Shake that shit. Strain into a highball glass with crushed ice. Top up with soda water. Garnish with the mint sprig and serve with a straw.

NOTES & VARIATIONS

A dash or two of Angostura bitters is a popular addition to the classic formula. Try adding fresh ginger, passion fruit, or pineapple to the muddle.

Replacing soda water with dry sparkling wine is a good move, if you're feeling posh. For bonus points, try a flavored sparkling water—passion fruit or pamplemousse, perhaps?

Daiquiri

The daiquiri has a bad reputation. But so do a lot of fucking interesting people in life! Who hasn't made some questionable choices in the past? The perfect drink to toast your own triumphant comeback.

Method

In an ice-filled cocktail shaker, combine the rum, lime juice, and simple syrup. Shake. Strain into a chilled coupe glass. Garnish with the lime wheel.

2 oz [60 ml] white rum

1 oz [30 ml] fresh lime juice

¾ oz [22 ml] simple syrup (page 18)

Lime wheel, for garnish

NOTES & VARIATIONS

Hemingway Daiquiri: Reduce the lime juice to ½ oz [15 ml] and add ½ oz [15 ml] fresh grapefruit juice. Reduce the simple syrup to ½ oz [15 ml] and add ¼ oz [7.5 ml] maraschino liqueur.

Floridita-Style Daiquiri: Reduce the lime juice to ½ oz [15 ml] and add [15 ml] fresh orange juice. Replace the simple syrup with Triple Sec.

Piña Colada

Some drinks just evoke something beyond the everyday. Chances are good you don't live in paradise—maybe no such place exists, but the feeling does. Cheers to your tropical escape!

½ cup [70 g] diced pineapple, frozen

2 oz [60 ml] rum, light or aged

1½ oz [45 ml] cream of coconut

1 oz [30 ml] pineapple juice

½ oz [15 ml] fresh lime juice

Pinch of salt

Maraschino cherry, for garnish

Pineapple wedge, for garnish

Straw, to serve

Method

Freeze the pineapple overnight if required. In a blender, combine the frozen pineapple, 1 cup [120 g] of ice cubes, the rum, cream of coconut, pineapple juice, lime juice, and salt. Blend until smooth. Serve in a hurricane glass, pint glass, or—if you're feeling the vibes—a frozen, hollowed-out pineapple. Garnish with the maraschino cherry, pineapple wedge, and a paper parasol, and serve with a straw.

NOTES & VARIATIONS

Since the pineapple is frozen and blended, use whichever form is most convenient for you. Pre-frozen, fresh, or canned (and drained) pineapple will all work, but canned in syrup will be notably sweeter.

Cream of coconut differs from coconut milk or cream; see page 22 for an alternative.

Fog Cutter

This tiki drink is strong as hell and a little over the top in a kitschy way. You probably shouldn't slam one at your desk at work to celebrate your promotion. It would, however, be the ideal way to toast your early retirement.

Method

In an ice-filled cocktail shaker, combine the rum, brandy, gin, orange juice, lemon juice, and orgeat. Shake well. Pour into a tiki mug with crushed ice or an ice-filled Collins glass. Float the sherry on top. Garnish with the mint sprig and serve with a straw.

1½ oz [45 ml] white rum or rhum agricole

½ oz [15 ml] brandy

½ oz [15 ml] gin

2 oz [60 ml] fresh orange juice

1 oz [30 ml] fresh lemon juice

½ oz [15 ml] orgeat (page 19)

½ oz [15 ml] amontillado sherry

Mint sprig, for garnish

Straw, to serve

NOTES & VARIATIONS

For more punch and less juice, replace the orange juice with ½ oz [15 ml] orange curaçao.

Cosmopolitan

Sometimes you want a drink that's pink as fuck. Sure, the Cosmo may have fallen out of fashion, but it certainly doesn't have a stick up its ass! Shake one up for yourself on a night when you're not trying to impress anyone, just enjoying yourself! We won't tell.

Method

In an ice-filled cocktail shaker, combine the vodka, Triple Sec, lime juice, and cranberry juice. Shake. Strain into a chilled martini glass or, if you're new-school, an ice-filled rocks glass. Garnish with the lime wedge.

1½ oz [45 ml] vodka (plain or citron flavored)

¾ oz [22 ml] Triple Sec

¾ oz [22 ml] fresh lime juice

1 oz [30 ml] cranberry juice

Lime wedge, for garnish

NOTES & VARIATIONS

Rude Cosmo: Replace the vodka with tequila and add 2 dashes of Angostura bitters.

Brazilian Cosmo: Replace the vodka with cachaça.

Pomsmo: Replace the cranberry juice with pomegranate juice.

Moscow Mule

Spicy ginger, zesty lime, and vodka make easy bedfellows, like a ménage à trois without the drama. It's no wonder it quickly rose to stardom when it was invented in 1940s Hollywood. Drink it and you'll feel like a star, too.

2 oz [60 ml] vodka

½ oz [15 ml] fresh lime juice

1 dash Angostura bitters (optional)

4 oz [120 ml] ginger ale

Lime wheel, for garnish

Mint sprig, for garnish

Method

In an ice-filled cocktail shaker, combine the vodka, lime juice, and bitters (if using). Shake. Strain into an ice-filled Collins glass or (if you're fancy as fuck) copper mule cup. Top with ginger ale. Garnish with the lime wheel and mint sprig.

NOTES & VARIATIONS

Horsefeather: Replace the vodka with whiskey.

Gin-Gin Mule: Replace the vodka with gin.

Mexican Mule: Replace the vodka with tequila.

CLASSY AS FUCK COCKTAILS

Bee's Knees

A Prohibition-era classic. Savor good times with the golden sweetness of this honey-based tipple. Its elegant simplicity makes it an effortless drink from the back porch to a sophisticated soirée.

Method

In an ice-filled cocktail shaker, combine the gin, honey syrup, and lemon juice. Shake. Strain into a chilled coupe glass. Garnish with the lemon twist.

2 oz [60 ml] gin

¾ oz [22 ml] rich honey syrup (page 18)

¾ oz [22 ml] fresh lemon juice

Lemon twist, for garnish

NOTES & VARIATIONS

Honeysuckle: Replace the gin with white rum.

Honeybee: Replace the gin with dark rum.

Dry Martini

Damn it all, but you can't help but feel a little extra suave with a martini in hand. It's a drink so iconic it has a glass named for itself. Treat yourself to one to celebrate a job well done, or anytime you feel like a living legend.

½ oz [15 ml] dry vermouth

2½ oz [80 ml] gin or vodka

Olive or lemon twist, for garnish

Method

In an ice-filled mixing glass, combine the vermouth and gin. Stir. Strain into a chilled martini glass. Garnish with an olive or a lemon twist.

NOTES & VARIATIONS

In martini terms, the less vermouth to spirit, the drier. The typical range runs from bone-dry (only rinse the glass with vermouth) to equal parts vermouth and spirit.

Dirty Martini: Add ½ oz [15 ml] good-quality olive brine (preferably Sicilian).

Burnt Martini: Add a splash of peated whiskey.

Tuxedo: Replace the vermouth with fino sherry and add a dash of orange bitters.

Earl Grey MarTEAni

There's nothing more civilized than a cup of tea, except perhaps a glass of gin. Why must it be one or the other? This tea-infused gin cocktail is a great pick-me-up, then lay-me-down—preferably on a lush fainting couch.

Method

In an ice-filled cocktail shaker, combine the infused gin, lemon juice, simple syrup, and egg white. Shake hard. Double strain into a chilled martini or coupe glass. Garnish with the lemon twist.

Origin: Audrey Saunders at The Ritz, London, UK (2003).

NOTES & VARIATIONS

The egg white in this drink gives it a beautiful foamy head that's quite stunning and unusual in a martini glass.

Tea is often overlooked in cocktails for what it can bring to the table. Seek out a good tea shop and go smell and taste the different blends for yourself.

1½ oz [45 ml]
Earl Grey tea–infused gin (page 21)

¾ oz [22 ml]
fresh lemon juice

1 oz [30 ml] simple syrup (page 18)

1 fresh egg white (page 17)

Lemon twist, for garnish

Tom Collins / Gin Fizz

Sometimes a hard day calls out for a hard lemonade, and there's no shame in that. But if the occasion calls for a little more finesse, then a fizz cocktail will hit the same spot, just with greater panache.

Method

In an ice-filled cocktail shaker, combine the gin, lemon juice, and simple syrup. Shake.

Tom Collins: Strain into an ice-filled Collins glass and top with soda water. Garnish with the lemon slice.

Gin Fizz: Strain into a chilled highball glass (without ice) and top with soda water. Garnish with the lemon slice.

2 oz [60 ml] gin

1 oz [30 ml] fresh lemon juice

1 oz [30 ml] simple syrup (page 18)

Soda water, for topping

Lemon slice, for garnish

NOTES & VARIATIONS

The difference between these two drinks is ice and volume (the highball glass holding slightly less than a Collins). Confusing as fuck? Blame history.

Royal Gin Fizz: Add 1 small, fresh whole egg.

Silver Fizz: Add ½ oz [15 ml] fresh egg white.

Golden Fizz: Add 1 small, fresh egg yolk.

Always give the egg (page 17) a good dry shake (page 12) ahead of the other ingredients.

Pegu Club

A forgotten classic, remembered. Sometimes even the most precious things are lost to memory for a time, but when we're reunited, it feels so good. A fitting drink to toast reconnecting with old friends.

1½ oz [45 ml] gin

⅔ oz [20 ml] orange curaçao or Triple Sec

⅓ oz [10 ml] fresh lime juice

2 dashes Angostura bitters

2 dashes orange bitters

Lime twist, for garnish (optional)

Method

In an ice-filled cocktail shaker, combine the gin, orange curaçao, lime juice, and bitters. Shake. Strain into a chilled martini glass. Serve neat or garnish with the lime twist.

NOTES & VARIATIONS

Jasmine: Reduce the amount of Triple Sec to ¼ oz [7.5 ml]. Replace the lime juice with ¾ oz [22 ml] fresh lemon juice. Add ¼ oz [7.5 ml] Campari. Garnish with a lemon twist. *Origin:* Paul Harrington at Townhouse, Emeryville, CA (1990s).

Brandy Alexander

This is decadence. Like, draped in fucking velvet, lounging across a grand piano decadence. It's dessert and after-dinner drinks in one! A delicious end to an evening or a luxurious and festive winter warmer.

Method

In an ice-filled cocktail shaker, combine the brandy, chocolate liqueur, cream, and egg white (if using). Shake. Strain into a chilled coupe glass. Garnish with a dusting of freshly grated nutmeg.

1 oz [30 ml] brandy

1 oz [30 ml] chocolate liqueur

1 oz [30 ml] cream

½ oz [15 ml] fresh egg white (optional, page 17)

Freshly grated nutmeg, for garnish

NOTES & VARIATIONS

Try a tropical-inspired version by replacing brandy with aged rum, chocolate liqueur with banana liqueur, and dairy cream with coconut cream. Omit the egg to make it completely vegan-friendly.

Mississippi Punch

Sometimes a celebration needs a starter pistol. We can think of no finer party starter than this deceptively strong number from the 1860s. Sure, they might just have been getting electricity, but they knew how to fucking party!

1 tsp superfine sugar

½ oz [15 ml] fresh lemon juice

2 oz [60 ml] brandy

1 oz [30 ml] bourbon

1 oz [30 ml] dark rum

Lemon or orange slice, for garnish

Seasonal berries, for garnish

Method

In a cocktail shaker, stir together the sugar and lemon juice until the sugar dissolves. Add the brandy, bourbon, and rum to the shaker with ice. Shake. Strain into an ice-filled Collins glass. Garnish with the lemon or orange slice and seasonal berries.

NOTES & VARIATIONS

This recipe traditionally calls for French cognac specifically but, quite frankly, the good shit is always expensive. This drink will still be plenty delicious with a more budget-friendly brandy.

Aperol Spritz

Few things are more Italian or more evocative of summer than an Aperol Spritz You don't need to be admiring a resplendent sunset from your Tuscan villa to enjoy one, but it certainly couldn't hurt.

Method

In a wine glass with ice, add the wine, Aperol, and soda water. Stir gently to combine. Garnish with the orange slice.

3 oz [90 ml] dry sparkling wine

2 oz [60 ml] Aperol

1 oz [30 ml] soda water

Orange slice, for garnish

NOTES & VARIATIONS

Other Italian amari, like Cappelletti or Montenegro or even Britain's favorite, Pimm's No. 1, all make delicious substitutions for Aperol to make an alternative spritz.

Try replacing sparkling wine with ginger ale, rhubarb soda, or bitter lemon.

La Dolce Fucking Vita

Aperol Mist

Cocktails or beer? Why choose when you can enjoy the best of both worlds? The Italian Riviera meets the poolside appeal of a fragrant Hefeweizen in this easy and appealing thirst slayer.

Method

In a pint glass with ice, combine the Aperol and lemon juice. Stir. Add beer and stir gently. Taste and add more lemon juice if desired. Garnish with the lemon peel.

1 oz [30 ml] Aperol

½ oz [15 ml]
fresh lemon juice

One 11.6 oz [330 ml]
bottle wheat beer

Lemon peel,
for garnish

NOTES & VARIATIONS

Belgian-style wheat beer is de rigueur for this drink, but any light, aromatic beer can work (even low-alcohol or near-beers). Aggressively hoppy IPAs can be difficult to balance with other ingredients.

Frozé

From the fanciest shaved ice to the humble slushie, there's an ineffable appeal to a frozen treat. Bonus points for being easy to make, delicious, and pink. This drink is an excellent pool party companion.

4 oz [120 ml] rosé wine

1½ oz [45 ml] pink grapefruit juice

½ oz [15 ml] Aperol

2 dashes pomegranate bitters (optional)

Mint sprig, for garnish

Method

In a blender, combine 1 cup [120 g] of ice cubes, wine, grapefruit juice, Aperol, and bitters (if using). Blend until incorporated. Pour into a double rocks glass and garnish with the mint sprig.

NOTES & VARIATIONS

Adjust the bitterness to your taste. If you prefer more bitter, replace the Aperol with Campari. If you prefer less bitter, replace the Aperol with Triple Sec.

If it's available where you live, 1 oz [30 ml] sloe gin makes a fantastic addition to this wine slushie and fits the color scheme to a T.

Mimosa

There is no better quaff than the mimosa to revel in the daylight hours. When you think about it, there really is no wrong time to be drinking Champagne. It's no wonder the mimosa bestrides the brunch bar like a colossus.

Method

In a wine glass with ice cubes, add the orange juice, then the sparkling wine. Stir well. Garnish with the orange slice.

3 oz [90 ml] orange juice

3 oz [90 ml] dry sparkling wine

Orange slice, for garnish

NOTES & VARIATIONS

Any sparkling wine will work well for this cocktail. Italian Prosecco and Spanish Cava tend to be more budget-friendly than French Champagne.

Buck's Fizz: Reduce orange juice to 2 oz [60 ml], raise sparkling wine to 4 oz [120 ml], and serve without ice.

Grand Mimosa: Reduce orange juice to 1½ oz [45 ml], add ¾ oz [22ml] Triple Sec, and serve with ice.

Bellini

There's something inexplicably romantic about Champagne. The addition of perfectly ripe fruit is an easy and elegant twist. Clink a glass with your sweetheart to celebrate a romantic anniversary. Or if you're single, salute yourself for being a damn fine catch!

1 oz [30 ml] white peach purée

5 oz [150 ml] dry sparkling wine

White peach purée

4 ripe white peaches, skins and pits removed

1½ oz [37 g] superfine sugar

Method

Make the peach purée ahead. Add the peach purée to a chilled Champagne flute. Top with sparkling wine. Stir gently.

To make the purée

In a blender, combine peaches, ½ cup [120 ml] water, and sugar. Blend until smooth. Strain into an airtight container. Refrigerate for up to 1 week.

NOTES & VARIATIONS

For best results, make the purée from scratch, but ready-made peach purée or nectar will do in a pinch.

Other stone fruits such as plums and apricots make great Bellini variations. Any seasonal fruits can work; try strawberry, mango, or kiwi.

When Life's a Bitch

Unwind with these stiff drinks and slow sippers

Some days are fucking golden, from the moment we spring out of bed, ready to kick ass and take names, to the moment we drift off to savor the sweet slumber of the truly blessed.

Then there are other days. Days where you feel like life's punching bag, and life decided to take kickboxing lessons after work. Easing that suck sometimes seems futile—there are no magic "fix-all-my-fucking-problems" potions.

But remember: If life is treating you like shit, that doesn't mean you should too. Give yourself a fucking break.

Put on a steaming hot bath, throw on your favorite tune, and if it feels right, pour a delicious drink. Sit back, take a deep breath, and remember there will be other days. Today might be a write-off, but that doesn't prove anything about tomorrow or the next day, or someday.

So until those magic potions are invented, here are a few suggested recipes to hold you over.

Tequila Sunrise

A 1970s throwback that's due for a revival, this cocktail is easy to make and easy on the eyes. One of those simple pleasures to help you decompress after a difficult day.

¼ oz [7.5 ml] grenadine (page 19 or see Note)

1½ oz [45 ml] tequila

3 oz [90 ml] orange juice

Orange wheel, for garnish

Cherry, for garnish

Method

In a chilled Collins glass, add the grenadine, top with ice, and set aside. In an ice-filled shaker Combine the tequila and orange juice. Shake. Gently strain into the Collins glass to maintain distinct layers. Garnish with the orange wheel and cherry.

NOTES & VARIATIONS

Contemporary palates can find the classic recipe a little oversweet—you may prefer to replace the grenadine with ½ oz [15 ml] crème de cassis (for a fruity tartness) or Campari (for bittersweetness).

Vampiro

The world can be a real vampire at times. Garlic and silver crosses might not be effective against its fangs, but at least there's tequila. This bubbly citrus and tequila drink will help things suck a little less.

Method

Make the sangrita ahead. In an ice-filled cocktail shaker, combine the sangrita, tequila, and lime juice. Shake. Strain into a double rocks glass with ice. Top with grapefruit soda and stir gently. Garnish with the lime or blood orange wedge.

To make sangrita

In a container big enough to hold at least 2 cups [480 ml], combine all the ingredients and stir. Refrigerate for up to 1 week. Serve leftovers as a chaser with tequila.

3 oz [90 ml] sangrita

1½ oz [45 ml] tequila

½ oz [15 ml] fresh lime juice

1½ oz [45 ml] grapefruit soda

Lime or blood orange wedge, for garnish

Sangrita

¾ cup [180 ml] orange juice

3 oz [90 ml] fresh lime juice

2 oz [60 ml] grenadine (page 19)

½ oz [15 ml] hot sauce

Mai Tai

A classic of the tiki genre, but not too daunting, the mai tai is a daiquiri on an island vacation. This is the drink you want when you want to be in a better place, even if just until the bottom of the glass.

2 oz [60 ml] gold rum

¾ oz [22 ml] fresh lime juice

½ oz [15 ml] orange curaçao

¼ oz [7.5 ml] rich simple syrup (page 18)

½ oz [7.5 ml] orgeat (page 19)

Mint sprig, for garnish

Method

In an ice-filled shaker, combine the rum, lime juice, curaçao, simple syrup, and orgeat. Shake vigorously. Strain into a rocks glass filled with crushed ice. Garnish with the mint sprig.

Origin: Victor "Trader Vic" Bergeron at Trader Vic's, Emeryville, CA (1944).

NOTES & VARIATIONS

If your home bar is not extensive, go for a single aged gold rum, preferably Jamaican. If you're keen to replicate the original recipe (which used a short-lived, unique rum), replace 1 oz [30 ml] of the rum with rhum agricole for added complexity.

Stone Fence

Invented during the American Revolutionary War, the Stone Fence is perfect if you're looking for your own liquid courage or something to quaff after your own hard-won battles.

Method

In an ice-filled Collins glass, combine the rum and bitters. Top off with cider and stir. Garnish with the mint sprig.

2 oz [60 ml] dark rum

1 or 2 dashes Angostura bitters

Hard apple cider, for topping

Mint sprig, for garnish

NOTES & VARIATIONS

Most dark spirits work in place of rum in this recipe. American whiskeys such as rye and bourbon stay closer to the drink's roots, but Scotch or brandy complements equally well. Cinnamon whiskey brings a wonderfully autumnal, warming apple pie note.

Bloody Mary

There are mornings when a coffee isn't going to cut it. Unfortunately, a Manhattan with eggs and toast is a look that few of us can pull off. Thankfully, there's the Bloody Mary, breakfast of champions.

2 oz [60 ml] vodka

4 oz [120 ml] tomato juice

½ oz [15 ml] fresh lemon juice

4 to 8 dashes hot sauce

4 dashes Worcestershire sauce

Pinch of freshly ground black pepper

Pinch of celery salt

Small celery stalk or lime wedge, for garnish

Method

In an ice-filled shaker, combine the vodka, juices, and sauces. Roll to mix and chill. Taste and adjust for seasoning, and then reroll. Strain into a Collins glass with ice. Dust with black pepper and celery salt. Garnish with the celery stalk (if you're old-school) or the lime wedge. *Please leave the whole rotisserie chicken and deep-fried cheeseburgers to Instagram. It's a garnish, not a fucking smorgasbord.*

NOTES & VARIATIONS

The backbone of the Bloody Mary isn't the booze; it's the balance of other ingredients. Think like a chef—taste and adjust. Watch for acidity, saltiness, and spice, and adjust the lemon juice, Worcestershire sauce, and hot sauce to balance.

Bloody Maria: Replace the vodka with tequila.

CLASSY AS FUCK COCKTAILS

Espresso Martini

The espresso martini is the total package. It picks you up with a caffeine hit and soothes your nerves with a gentle caress of vodka. It's like the best friend character in a good romcom, but in a glass.

Method

In an ice-filled cocktail shaker, combine the vodka, espresso, and coffee liqueur. Shake with gusto. Strain into a chilled martini glass. Float coffee beans on top to garnish.

Origin: Dick Bradsell at Soho Brasserie, London (1983).

1½ oz [45 ml] vodka

1 oz [30 ml] espresso

¾ oz [22 ml] coffee liqueur

3 coffee beans, for garnish

NOTES & VARIATIONS

With this drink, the quality of the coffee will make the difference between it being *the shit* or just shit. Use fresh hot espresso or, alternatively, a concentrated form of cold brew (you will need to dilute to taste, as concentrates vary in strength).

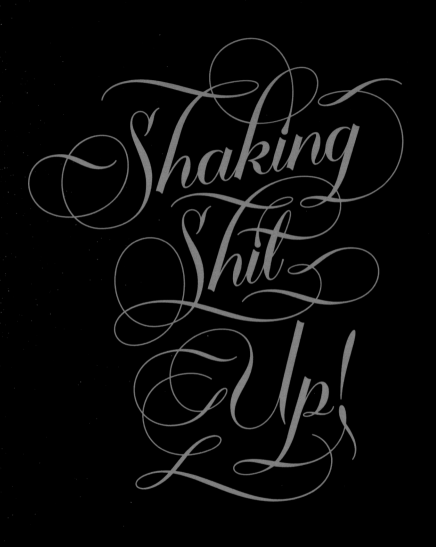

White Russian

Say somebody came into your place and ruined a piece of decor that really tied the room together—which drink would you reach for? Something decadent and sumptuous, of course. It may or may not help you recover your zen, but it'll be fucking delicious regardless.

1 oz [30 ml] vodka

1 oz [30 ml] coffee liqueur

1½ oz [45 ml] cream

Method

In an ice-filled cocktail shaker, combine the vodka, coffee liqueur, and cream. Shake until well chilled. Pour into a rocks glass with ice.

NOTES & VARIATIONS

Optionally, adding ¼ oz [7.5 ml] of cold-brew coffee concentrate will boost the coffee note.

Some prefer to shake only the vodka and coffee liqueur and layer the cream, whipped to soft peaks, on top. Use anything from half-and-half to heavy cream, depending on your level of decadence. Coconut cream can also be used for a vegan alternative.

Dirty Russian: Replace the cream with chocolate milk.

Black Russian: Omit the cream altogether.

Gin & Tonic

Mel & Sue, Fry & Laurie, empire & exploitation. It's hard to name a more iconic British double act than the effervescent G&T and bloody well impossible to find one that has aged better.

2 oz [60 ml] gin

Tonic water, for topping

Lime wedge, for garnish

Method

In an ice-filled highball glass, add the gin. Top with tonic water. Stir to mix. Garnish with the lime wedge.

NOTES & VARIATIONS

Wanker's Delight: Add ½ oz [15 ml] elderflower liqueur, 1 oz [30 ml] grapefruit juice, and 2 dashes Angostura bitters. *Origin:* The Bill Murray pub, London (2017).

In Normandy, France, apple brandy is mixed with tonic, while in Porto, Portugal they prefer white port (naturally). For a different take, replace the gin with white or dark rum and a generous squeeze of lime.

Salty Dog

Gin and juice is a winning combination—like Snoop and Dre, or Snoop and Martha Stewart. Whether you have your mind on your money or muffins on your mind, just take a sip and get laid back.

Method

In an ice-filled highball glass, combine the gin, juice, and a pinch of salt. Stir. Add the bitters and garnish with the lemon or grapefruit wedge.

2 oz [60 ml] gin

6 oz [180 ml] fresh grapefruit juice

Pinch of fine-grain salt

2 dashes orange bitters

Lemon or grapefruit wedge, for garnish

NOTES & VARIATIONS

Traditionally this drink is served with a salt rim, but we suggest you add a dash directly to the drink.

Salty Chihuahua: Replace the gin with tequila, mezcal, or a blend of both.

Corpse Reviver No. 2

This is a vintage potion for necromancy from the golden age of cocktails. Take heed of the warning inscribed in its first written recipe: *Four of these taken in swift succession will unrevive the corpse again.*

¾ oz [22 ml] gin

¾ oz [22 ml] Triple Sec

¾ oz [22 ml] Lillet Blanc or Cocchi Americano

¾ oz [22 ml] fresh lemon juice

1 dash absinthe or anise liqueur

Orange peel, for garnish (optional)

Method

In an ice-filled cocktail shaker, combine the gin, Triple Sec, Lillet Blanc, lemon juice, and absinthe. Shake it like you mean it. Strain into a chilled coupe glass. Garnish with the orange peel, if desired.

Origin: Harry Craddock at Savoy Hotel, London (circa 1930).

Suffering Bastard

This bourbon- and gin-based classic was invented as a hangover "cure." The veracity of the medical claims may be questionable, but there's only one way to test if it will ease your burden. Luckily, drinking it is no hard slog.

Method

In an ice-filled cocktail shaker, combine the bourbon, gin, lime juice, and bitters. Shake like the dickens. Strain into an ice-filled rocks glass. Top with ginger ale and garnish with the mint sprig.

Origin: Joe Scialom at Shepheard's Hotel, Cairo, Egypt (1942).

NOTES & VARIATIONS

This drink was the first part of a trilogy of "bastard" drinks created by Joe Scialom in the mid-twentieth century. The second, the *Dying Bastard*, uses 1 oz [30 ml] each of both bourbon and brandy instead of one or the other, in addition to the gin. The final, *Dead Bastard*, uses 4 oz [120 ml] of spirits: equal parts bourbon, brandy, gin, and white rum.

1 oz [30 ml] bourbon or brandy

1 oz [30 ml] gin

½ oz [15 ml] fresh lime juice

2 dashes Angostura bitters

Ginger ale, for topping

Mint sprig, for garnish

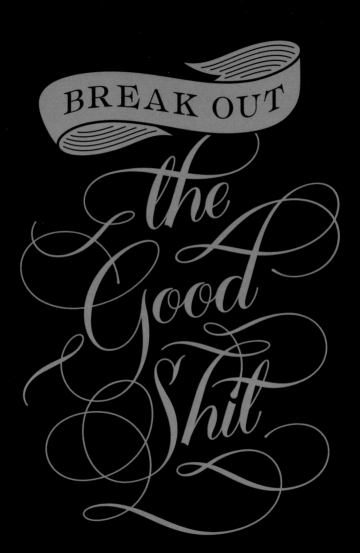

Old Fashioned

When the day hands you your ass, you don't have energy to deal with bullshit. Things don't get more no-nonsense than the old fashioned. Whiskey with a bittersweet edge, it's 100 percent bullshit-free.

Method

In a rocks glass, combine the sugar, bitters, and a splash of warm water. Muddle until the sugar dissolves. Add the whiskey and a big-ass, beautiful ice cube. Stir. Garnish with the orange peel.

1 cube or 1 tsp sugar

2 or 3 dashes Angostura bitters

2 oz [60 ml] bourbon or rye whiskey

Orange peel, for garnish

NOTES & VARIATIONS

Many cocktails will do fine with less than top-shelf liquor. It can even be a shame to use the really good stuff where the nuances get lost in the mix. The old fashioned is not one of those cases. Use the good shit.

Sazerac: Use rye whiskey only, replace Angostura with Peychaud's bitters, and serve in an absinthe-washed glass with a lemon peel garnish.

Manhattan

No matter what's bringing you down, the Manhattan is a drink that's easy to love. It's the liquid equivalent of the borough's great parts, minus the subway rats, the tourist traps, and the fucking ego.

2 oz [60 ml] bourbon or rye whiskey

1 oz [30 ml] sweet vermouth

2 dashes Angostura bitters

Brandied cherry, for garnish

Method

In an ice-filled mixing glass, combine the whiskey, vermouth, and bitters. Stir to chill. Strain into a chilled martini or coupe glass. Garnish with the brandied cherry.

NOTES & VARIATIONS

The Manhattan can also be built and served in a rocks glass, if you're so inclined.

Reverse Manhattan: Switch the ratio of whiskey to vermouth: 1 oz [30 ml] whiskey to 2 oz [60 ml] vermouth.

Dry Manhattan: Replace the sweet vermouth with dry vermouth, and replace the cherry with a lemon twist.

CLASSY AS FUCK COCKTAILS

Rusty Nail

In classic films, you can tell someone's had a shit day when they order Scotch on the rocks. Despite its name, the Rusty Nail is a smoother variation with herbal honey liqueur rounding out some of the edge. Sip it in a dark office with the blinds drawn.

Method

In a rocks glass with a large ice cube, combine the Scotch, Drambuie, and bitters (if using). Stir. Garnish with the lemon twist.

2 oz [60 ml]
blended Scotch

¾ oz [22 ml]
Drambuie

1 dash Angostura
bitters (optional)

Lemon twist,
for garnish

NOTES & VARIATIONS

The ratio of ingredients in this drink ranges widely. If you find this too sweet for your taste, halve the volume of Drambuie or add Scotch if already mixed.

Smoky Nail: Replace the blended Scotch with peated Scotch or a fifty-fifty mix of both whiskeys.

Godfather: Replace the Drambuie with amaretto.

Whiskey Sour

When life gives you lemons, make a whiskey sour. It's simple, delicious, and has fewer calories than lemonade. Plus, after enough of them, you won't even remember who gave you the fucking lemons anyway.

2 oz [60 ml] bourbon or rye whiskey

¾ oz [22 ml] fresh lemon juice

¾ oz [22 ml] simple syrup (page 18)

½ oz [15 ml] fresh egg white (optional, page 17)

2 or 3 dashes Angostura bitters (optional)

Orange slice, for garnish

Maraschino cherry, for garnish

Method

In an ice-filled cocktail shaker, combine the whiskey, lemon juice, simple syrup, egg white (if using), and bitters (if using). Shake. Strain into an ice-filled rocks or coupe glass. Garnish with the orange slice and maraschino cherry skewered on a stick.

NOTES & VARIATIONS

New York Sour: Add a float of ¾ oz [22 ml] red wine on top. Known by damn too many other names.

Amaretto Sour: Replace the whiskey with amaretto and omit the simple syrup.

Gold Rush: Replace the simple syrup with rich honey syrup (page 18).

CLASSY AS FUCK COCKTAILS

Whiskey Smash

Building on the sour formula, the smash is satisfying and damn refreshing. Let the mint leaves take the brunt of your frustrations with a muddler and some elbow grease, then let it chill your nerves as you sip.

Method

In the bottom of a cocktail shaker or mixing glass, muddle the mint leaves and simple syrup to release the mint's essential oils. Add ice, bourbon, and lemon juice. Shake until well chilled. Strain into an ice-filled rocks glass. Garnish with the mint sprig.

6 large mint leaves

½ oz [15 ml] simple syrup (page 18)

2 oz [60 ml] bourbon

½ oz [15 ml] fresh lemon juice

Mint sprig, for garnish

NOTES & VARIATIONS

To make a *Mint Julep* for the Kentucky Derby or any other fancy occasion, follow the same recipe as the smash but omit the lemon juice and build in a silver julep cup with crushed ice.

Alternative spirits to try in either a smash or a julep include rye or other whiskey, brandy, and dark rum.

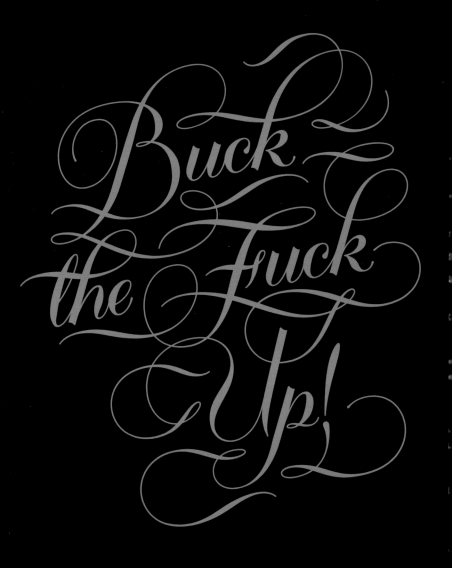

Penicillin

The medicinal properties of ginger and honey go back to antiquity, but this modern take on the whiskey sour has become an instant classic. The spice of ginger and the smoky aroma will do wonders for whatever ails you.

Method

In an ice-filled cocktail shaker, combine the blended Scotch, honey-ginger syrup, and lemon juice. Shake. Strain into an ice-filled rocks glass. Float the peated Scotch on top. Garnish with the candied ginger.

Origin: Sam Ross at Milk & Honey, New York City (2005).

2 oz [60 ml]
blended Scotch

¾ oz [22 ml]
honey-ginger syrup
(page 18)

¾ oz [22 ml]
fresh lemon juice

¼ oz [7.5 ml]
peated Scotch

Candied ginger,
for garnish

Highball

Simplicity is a virtue, especially when you're beat down and thirsty. The highball has got your fucking back. Straightforward, delicious, and endlessly adaptable to whatever you have at hand. What else do you need?

2 oz [60 ml] bourbon or rye whiskey

Soda water, for topping

Lemon slice, for garnish

Method

In an ice-filled highball glass, add the whiskey. Top with soda water. Stir to mix. Garnish with the lemon slice.

NOTES & VARIATIONS

Replace whiskey with any spirit, dark or light. Alternative carbonated mixers include ginger ale, bitter lemon, tonic water, or flavored seltzer.

Japanese Highball: Use Japanese instead of American whiskey and no garnish.

Gin Buck: Use gin instead of whiskey, ginger ale instead of soda water, and a lemon wedge instead of a lemon slice.

Hot Toddy

The weather outside is wet, cold, and miserable, and consequently, so are you. Few things can warm your soul and disposition like a hot toddy. Sure, there's chicken soup, but who wants chicken when there's whiskey?

Method

Preheat a mug or heatproof glass with hot water, then discard the water. Add the honey, lemon juice, and whiskey, topping up with boiling water. Stir until honey is dissolved. Add the lemon wheel and cinnamon stick directly to the drink and stir gently.

NOTES & VARIATIONS

If using tea for topping, brew in a mug or teapot separately before assembling the toddy so that it doesn't become over-steeped and astringent.

For a spiced variation, try using an herbal tea and pairing it with a liqueur like sambuca (anise), aquavit (caraway), or ouzo (anise) in lieu of the whiskey.

2 tsp honey or brown sugar

½ oz [15 ml] fresh lemon juice

2 oz [60 ml] bourbon or rye whiskey

Boiling water or tea, for topping

Lemon wheel

Cinnamon stick

Black Velvet

The Black Velvet was invented for the somber occasion of the death of Prince Albert, as it was decided that to be seen drinking Champagne would have been unacceptable, given the atmosphere. It's the classic choice for a miserable occasion or St. Patrick's Day.

Black stout beer

¼ oz [7.5 ml] blackcurrant liqueur (optional)

Dry sparkling wine, for topping

Method

Fill a chilled Collins glass, pint glass, or Champagne flute halfway with stout beer. If desired, add blackcurrant liqueur. Top with dry sparkling wine. Stir gently.

Origin: Brooks's Club, London (1861).

NOTES & VARIATIONS

Guinness is the most famous black stout beer, though any dark stout or porter-style beer will work.

The drier the sparkling wine, the better. Another variation is to replace sparkling wine with dry apple cider—Spanish sidra works particularly well.

Batch-Shit Crazy

Punches and other make-ahead batch drinks

Two's company. Three's a crowd. Four or more is either a meeting— or a party, if there are drinks. Regardless of your background, color or creed, we can all universally agree on one thing: the last thing the world needs is more fucking meetings.

If you want to host a cocktail party, and not be the *bartender* at said cocktail party, it helps to prepare drinks by the batch. That way you get to spend more time eating, drinking, and merry-making instead of pulling a late shift behind the bar.

Unless you have a staff of dozens, a carefully chosen, limited selection of drinks is perfect. One or two batch cocktails, beer, wine, and alcohol-free options—and you're all set.

So invite your nearest and dearest, or just the people you want to hang out with more often—whip up a batch or two of excellent drinks before the celebrations start, and pour them a glass as they come through the door.

Or set out a punch bowl and let them help themselves. Now that's a kind of self-help anyone can get behind!

Watermelon Cooler

Makes 10 servings

Vessel: Watermelon bowl or 12 cup [2.8 L] or larger pitcher

6 to 8 lb [2.7 to 3.6 kg] seedless watermelon

One 750 ml bottle tequila

½ cup [120 ml] fresh lime juice

½ cup [120 ml] simple syrup or habañero syrup (page 18)

½ tsp fine-grain salt

10 mint sprigs, for garnish

There's just no question what kind of gathering you're at when you see a watermelon filled with booze. It's not jury duty, that's for damn sure. This is the best possible way to tell people summer has arrived.

Method

To make a watermelon bowl:
Slice ½ in [10 mm] of rind from the bottom to allow the melon to sit upright, then slice a lid 2 in [5 cm] from the top.

Working in batches, scoop out the flesh from the interior of the watermelon and purée in a blender. Strain through a sieve. In the watermelon bowl or pitcher, combine the watermelon purée, tequila, lime juice, simple syrup, and salt. Refrigerate for at least 2 hours.

To serve, pour into ice-filled Collins glasses. Garnish with the mint sprigs.

Mezcal Paloma

Grapefruit is a great base for a cocktail, because it brings bitter, sweet, and sour to your drink single-handedly. This version adds smoky complexity with mezcal and charred rosemary, because why not add a little fucking drama?

Method

In a pitcher, add salt and a few ice cubes. Stir until the salt dissolves. Add the tequila, mezcal, and grapefruit soda. Stir.

To serve, pour into ice-filled Collins glasses. For the garnish, briefly ignite the tips of a rosemary sprig with a blowtorch or kitchen lighter, immediately blow out, and set into the drink while still smoldering.

NOTES & VARIATIONS

This recipe uses a mix of tequila and mezcal but works great if you use only one or the other.

For more bitter complexity, add 1 oz [30 ml] of Campari to the mix, or add 1 or 2 dashes Angostura or grapefruit bitters per glass.

Makes 8 servings

Vessel: 8 cup [2 L] or larger pitcher

½ tsp fine-grain salt

1 cup [240 ml] tequila

1 cup [240 ml] mezcal

4 cups [960 ml] grapefruit soda

8 rosemary sprigs, for garnish

Fish House Punch

This two-hundred-year-old recipe comes from Colonial Philadelphia. Don't underestimate its strength and drinkability, or this fresh punch might have you going from maxing and relaxing to starting trouble in the neighborhood.

Makes 8 servings

Vessel: 8 cup [2 L] or larger punch bowl

Peel of 1 lemon

½ cup [100 g] brown sugar

1½ cups [360 ml] weak black tea or hot water

1½ cups [360 ml] dark rum

6 oz [180 ml] brandy

6 oz [180 ml] peach brandy or peach liqueur

6 oz [180 ml] fresh lemon juice

Punch ice (page 16 or see Note)

8 lemon wheels, for garnish

Freshly grated nutmeg, for garnish

Method

In a punch bowl, add the lemon peel and sugar. Muddle well and let sit for 30 minutes to release the citrus oil. Add tea and mix until the sugar dissolves. Remove lemon peel and add the rum, brandies, and lemon juice. Stir well, cover, and refrigerate for at least 3 hours, until well chilled. Add the punch ice before serving.

To serve, ladle into punch cups. Garnish with the lemon wheels and a dusting of freshly grated nutmeg.

NOTES & VARIATIONS

This version is scaled at half a standard 700 or 750 ml rum bottle but can easily be doubled.

It can also be made in a pitcher with regular ice cubes, which, to be sure, is more practical but certainly lacks the old-world charm.

CLASSY AS FUCK COCKTAILS

Here's to a Damn

FINE DRINK

Pisco Punch

Despite being called a punch, this post-California Gold Rush concoction was originally served from behind a bar, not from a bowl. Pisco can be a little hard to come by, but is worth seeking out for a special celebration!

Makes 10 servings

Vessel: 7 cup [1.6 L] or larger pitcher

One 750 ml bottle pisco

1½ cups [360 ml] fresh pineapple juice

¾ cup [180 ml] fresh lime juice

½ cup [120 ml] rich simple syrup (page 18)

10 pineapple wedges, for garnish

Method

In a large pitcher, combine the pisco, juices, and simple syrup. Stir until well blended. Refrigerate for at least 2 hours.

To serve, pour into ice-filled rocks or punch glasses. Garnish with the pineapple wedges.

Origin: The Bank Exchange Saloon, San Francisco (circa 1870s).

NOTES & VARIATIONS

This can also be served as a long drink in ice-filled Collins glasses and topped with mineral water, coconut water, Agua de Piña (page 107), or Tepache de Piña (page 107).

Bottled Negroni

When you're hosting at short notice, it's comforting to have something that's almost impossible to fuck up. Enter the Negroni. Three equal parts, build it in the glass or by the bottle—glorious.

Method

Using a funnel, add the gin, Campari, and vermouth to a 750 ml wine bottle. Cap and roll the bottle to mix. Refrigerate for at least 2 hours.

To serve, pour into ice-filled rocks glasses. Garnish with the orange wedges.

NOTES & VARIATIONS

Boulevardier: Replace the gin with bourbon.

Old Pal: Replace the gin with rye whiskey, and replace the sweet vermouth with dry vermouth.

Americano: Omit the gin, and top each serving with soda water.

Makes 10 servings

Vessel: Standard 750 ml wine bottle

1 cup [240 ml] gin

1 cup [240 ml] Campari

1 cup [240 ml] sweet vermouth

10 orange wedges, for garnish

Pimm's Cup

The Pimm's Cup is a storied British summer institution along with Wimbledon, beer gardens, fish and chips by the seaside, and having two weeks of glorious sunshine before it starts pissing down with rain again.

Makes 12 servings

Vessel: 12 cup [2.8 L] or larger pitcher

700 ml bottle Pimm's No. 1 (page 22)

One 2 L bottle lemon-lime soda or dry ginger ale

2 large oranges, sliced into thin wheels

12 large strawberries, hulled and quartered

12 mint sprigs, for garnish

12 curled cucumber peels, for garnish

Method

In a pitcher, add the Pimm's and lemon-lime soda. Stir gently to mix.

To serve, fill chilled Collins glasses with ice and fruit, distributing fruit throughout (aim for 1 or 2 orange wheels and 4 strawberry pieces per glass). Pour in the Pimm's mixture. Garnish with the mint sprigs and cucumber peels.

NOTES & VARIATIONS

This drink is also known as Pimms & Lemonade. Lemonade is what Brits call lemon-lime soda. Please don't use American lemonade in a Pimm's Cup.

Fluffy AF Eggnog

As the year comes to a close, you can decry the pumpkin-spiced fuckaccino all you like, but there's something to be said for a winter-spiced dessert in a glass. Homemade with booze in it, all the better!

Method

Separate the egg yolks from the whites and reserve. In a large mixing bowl, beat the egg whites with salt until frothy. Continue whipping while slowly adding ⅓ cup [65 g] of the sugar. Whisk to firm but not stiff peaks (around shaving cream consistency). Reserve.

Add the egg yolks to a bowl with the remaining ⅓ cup [65 g] sugar and whisk until pale. When you lift the whisk, the mixture should form ribbons that slowly dissolve into the batter. Slowly incorporate the brandy, then the heavy cream and milk.

Gently fold the reserved egg whites into the mixture. Refrigerate for at least 1 hour, or overnight.

To serve, gently mix before ladling into small wine glasses or cups. Garnish with freshly grated nutmeg.

Makes 10 servings

Vessel: 4 quart [3.8 L] or larger mixing bowl

8 fresh whole eggs (page 17)

Pinch of salt

⅔ cup [130 g] sugar

2 cups [480 ml] brandy, dark rum, or bourbon

1½ cup [360 ml] heavy cream

1½ cup [360 ml] whole milk

Freshly grated nutmeg, for garnish

Sangría

To talk batch drinks without mentioning sangría is like forgetting popcorn in a discussion of movie snacks or Earth when talking planets. It may seem fucking obvious, but sometimes that's just a sign of undeniable greatness.

Makes 8 servings

Vessel: 11 cup [2.6 L] or larger punch bowl

Method

Add fruit, sweetener, spirits, and juice to a large container. Mix well and let sit for 1 to 4 hours, or refrigerate overnight.

To serve, add the fruit mixture and wine to a large punch bowl with 4 cups [480 g] of ice. Ladle into wine glasses, taking care to distribute ice and fruit evenly. Top with the mixer and stir.

Serve with a bamboo skewer for your guests to better enjoy the boozy fruit (rather than tilting the glass and getting a fucking faceful).

Red	White	Rosé
FRUIT	**FRUIT**	**FRUIT**
1 orange, cut into thin wedges	2 kiwis, cubed	1 grapefruit, cut into thin wedges
1 lemon, cut into wheels	2 peaches or nectarines, pitted and sliced	½ cup [60 g] raspberries
1 apple, cored and cubed	1 pear, cored and cubed	½ cup [70 g] strawberries, sliced
SWEETENER	**SWEETENER**	**SWEETENER**
4 Tbsp [50 g] superfine sugar	4 Tbsp [85 g] honey	4 Tbsp [50 g] superfine sugar
SPIRITS	**SPIRITS**	**SPIRITS**
½ cup [120 ml] brandy or sherry	½ cup [120 ml] elderflower liqueur or cordial	½ cup [120 ml] Aperol
JUICE	**JUICE**	**JUICE**
½ cup [120 ml] orange juice	3 oz [90 ml] fresh lemon juice	3 oz [90 ml] fresh lemon juice
WINE	**WINE**	**WINE**
One 750 ml bottle red wine	One 750 ml bottle dry white wine	One 750 ml bottle sparkling rosé wine
MIXER	**MIXER**	**MIXER**
Soda water, for topping	Unsweetened, chilled white tea, for topping	Soda water, for topping

French 75 Punch

Some friends bring out the fucking best in each other—gin, citrus, and bubbles are one such trio. It's the kind of company we should all aspire to keep, and the perfect toasting cocktail. Here's to your health!

Method

In a punch bowl, combine the gin, lemon juice, simple syrup, and bitters. Stir until well mixed. Refrigerate until needed.

Before serving, add the punch ice and the sparkling wine. Gently stir. Ladle into ice-filled Champagne flutes or punch glasses and garnish with a long thin strip of lemon zest, twisted to express the essential oils over the drink.

NOTES & VARIATIONS

This can also be built in a large pitcher with regular ice cubes for ease of serving, though you definitely miss out on a certain *je ne sais quoi*.

French 76: Replace the gin or cognac with vodka.

French 77: Replace the simple syrup with ⅔ cup [160 ml] elderflower liqueur or cordial.

Makes 6 servings

Vessel: 8 cup [2 L] or larger punch bowl

1½ cup [360 ml] gin or cognac

4 oz [120 ml] fresh lemon juice

3 oz [90 ml] simple syrup (page 18)

½ tsp Angostura bitters or absinthe

Punch ice (page 16 or see Note)

One 750 ml bottle dry sparkling wine

6 lemon twists, for garnish

Mulled Wine & Cider

Makes 8 servings

Vessel: 8 cup [1.9 L] or larger saucepan or slow cooker

There are fewer things more comforting than a steaming cup of spiced hooch. It's little surprise that nearly every country in Northern Europe has its own variation on this cold-weather potion.

Method

In a saucepan or slow cooker, combine all the ingredients for the mulled beverage. If cooking on the stove top, bring to a low simmer (not a rolling boil) while stirring. Once simmering, turn off the heat and let sit for at least 20 minutes. Reheat before serving. If using a slow cooker, cover and cook on the low setting for 2 to 3 hours.

To serve, ladle into heatproof glasses, straining out any spices. Add the optional shot if desired, stirring to mix. Garnish with the cinnamon sticks and lemon wheels.

NOTES & VARIATIONS

For a zero-proof version, simply use a nonalcoholic wine or cider, or replace the red wine with 2 cups [480 ml] pomegranate juice and 1 cup [240 ml] black tea.

Red Wine	White Wine	Apple Cider
MULLED WINE	**MULLED WINE**	**MULLED CIDER**
1 Tbsp allspice berries	1 whole star anise pod	1 Tbsp allspice berries
1 whole star anise pod	1 thick slice fresh ginger, peeled	4 whole cloves
3 whole cloves	3 cardamom pods, bruised	2 cinnamon sticks, broken
2 cinnamon sticks, broken	4 Tbsp [85 g] honey	4 Tbsp [50 g] dark brown sugar
4 Tbsp [50 g] light brown sugar	One 750 ml bottle dry white wine	4 cups [960 ml] dry apple cider
One 750 ml bottle dry red wine		
OPTIONAL SHOT (PER SERVING)	**OPTIONAL SHOT (PER SERVING)**	**OPTIONAL SHOT (PER SERVING)**
½ oz [15 ml] brandy, whiskey, or Triple Sec	½ oz [15 ml] pear or apple brandy	½ oz [15 ml] brandy, spiced rum, or cinnamon whiskey
GARNISH (PER SERVING)	**GARNISH (PER SERVING)**	**GARNISH (PER SERVING)**
Cinnamon stick	Cinnamon stick	Cinnamon stick
Lemon wheel	Lemon wheel	Lemon wheel

Unabashedly Unshitfaced

Obscenely delicious low- and no-alcohol drinks

Avoiding alcohol does not equal avoiding fun! Being mindful about your drinking is admirable and takes fucking guts. With or without booze, everyone should be able to enjoy a delicious beverage with friends or for the pleasure of the drink itself.

This chapter covers beverages designed to be low- or no-alcohol. Instead of working backward from a boozy cocktail and swapping or subtracting, we're building in complexity of flavor through other means. It might seem like a small thing, but it means you or your guests get to enjoy the best version of these drinks.

Plus, an increasing number of "zero-proof spirits" (alcohol-free distilled infusions) are available, which can be substituted in classic cocktails. Often a straight substitution means no new recipe is needed, so we won't cover those here.

So, hold your head high and dry! These recipes are for one serving unless specified. But be warned, they taste so good, they'll make anybody sober-curious, or at least thirsty to give it a try. You might want to prepare them by the batch, just in case!

Grown-Ass Lemonade

This lemonade will put every six-year-old on the street out of business. Sweet and sour gets the addition of smoky, savory, and subtle spice. Tough shit, kids!

Makes 10 servings

Vessel: 7 cup [1.7 L] or larger pitcher

7 or 8 unwaxed lemons, sliced into ½ in [10 mm] wheels

½ cup [100 g] sugar

1 cup [340 g] honey

¼ tsp smoked sea salt or fine-grain salt

1 Tbsp black peppercorns, coarsely ground

Soda water, for topping (optional)

10 mint sprigs, for garnish

Method

Preheat the oven to 425°F [220°C] and line baking sheets with parchment paper. Sprinkle the lemon wheels with sugar on both sides. Place the lemons on the prepared baking sheets and bake for 15 to 20 minutes, until browned.

Let cool. Reserve and halve 5 of the wheels for garnish. Add 2 cups [480 ml] of water, the honey, salt, and pepper to a saucepan. Bring to a boil, stirring. Lower the heat and simmer for 5 minutes. Take off the heat and allow to cool. Squeeze the remaining lemons directly into pan and mix. Strain through a fine-mesh sieve into a large pitcher. Add 3 cups [720 ml] more water. Refrigerate for at least 2 hours.

To serve, pour into ice-filled Collins glasses. Top with soda water, if desired. Garnish with the reserved lemon wheel halves and the mint sprigs.

Coffee Soda

Not every recipe has to be a whole-day affair. This one can be sorted out with a quick run to the corner store. An effervescent and zesty pick-me-up and a wonderful alternative to a traditional iced coffee.

4 oz [120 ml] cold-brew coffee

¾ oz [22 ml] fresh lime juice

1 oz [30 ml] simple syrup (page 18)

4 oz [120 ml] soda water

Lemon twist, for garnish

Straw, to serve (optional)

Method

In an ice-filled cocktail shaker, combine the coffee, lime juice, and simple syrup. Shake well. Strain into an ice-filled Collins glass, top with soda water, and give a gentle stir. Garnish with the lemon twist and enjoy with or without a straw.

NOTES & VARIATIONS

Espresso can work in place of cold brew. Use 1 oz [30 ml] espresso and 6 oz soda water.

For low-alcohol variations, add 2 oz [60 ml] amontillado sherry or 1 oz [30 ml] Averna or other amaro.

Coffee Tonic: Replace the soda water with tonic water. Omit the lime and simple syrup.

Shrub Soda

Shrubs are surprisingly delicious vinegar syrups that bring depth and complexity to any mixed drink—with or without alcohol. They're hard to fuck up, easy to like and enjoyable year-round since they work with any seasonal fruit.

Method

In an ice-filled Collins glass, add the shrub and orgeat. Stir well. Top with soda water and bitters (if using). Mix gently to keep a visual gradient between the layers. Garnish with a thin slice of pear.

2 oz [60 ml] pear and fig shrub (page 20)

1 oz [30 ml] orgeat (page 19) or simple syrup (page 18)

5 oz [150 ml] soda water or dry ginger ale

2 dashes Peychaud's bitters (optional)

Pear slice, for garnish

NOTES & VARIATIONS

For a low-alcohol variation, add 1½ oz [45 ml] sake or soju.

Alternative shrub syrups (page 20):

· Nectarines, honey, and Champagne vinegar.

· Rhubarb and roasted strawberries, demerara sugar, and balsamic vinegar.

Aguas Frescas

You've got to hand it to Latin America: They know how to do liquid refreshment right. They dominate like Van Gogh in a finger-painting contest. Each agua fresca is a liquid master-piece and pure magic on a hot day.

Makes 6 servings

Vessel: 6 cup [1.4 L] or larger pitcher

Method

Agua de Jamaica/Piña: In a large pot over high heat, combine all the agua ingredients with 6 cups [1.4 L] of water. Bring to a boil, then lower the heat to low and simmer for 10 minutes. Let cool, then strain through a fine-mesh sieve. Transfer to a pitcher and refrigerate for at least 2 hours. Serve over ice in a tall glass. The aguas can be kept in the refrigerator for up to 5 days.

Horchata: In a blender, pulverize the rice. Add sugar, cinnamon, salt, and 4 cups [1 L] of water. Blend until smooth. Refrigerate overnight.

The next day, strain through a fine-mesh sieve. Combine with the milk in a large pitcher, taste, and adjust for sweetness. Serve over ice in a tall glass and garnish with a dusting of cinnamon.

Agua de Jamaica

1½ cup [100 g]
dried hibiscus
flowers, washed

2 tsp fresh grated
ginger (optional)

¾ cup [150 g] sugar

Agua de Piña

Core and well-
washed skin of
1 pineapple

½ tsp whole cloves

¾ cup [150 g] sugar

Horchata

1 cup [200 g]
uncooked
long-grain rice

¾ cup [150 g] sugar

1 tsp ground
cinnamon, plus
more for garnish

¼ tsp fine-grain salt

2 cups [240 ml] milk
or almond milk

NOTES & VARIATIONS

Tepache de Piña is a fermented version of Agua de Piña, with 1 to 3 percent ABV
depending on fermentation time.

In a sterile ceramic or glass vessel, mix together all the Agua de Piña ingredients and
cover with plastic wrap. Store in a cool, dark spot for 2 or 3 days, until it begins to
bubble. Remove the solids and strain through a coffee filter or cheesecloth into a clean
8 cup [2 L] jar. Keep refrigerated for up to 1 week.

Kombucha Crackler

Kombucha was once the exclusive fare of the bare-footed granola set. Not anymore, and why the fuck not? You don't need alternative ideas about crystals or hygiene to enjoy its zippy, tingly goodness!

Method

In an ice-filled cocktail shaker, combine the juices, orgeat, and bitters (if using). Shake. Strain into an ice-filled rocks glass. Top with kombucha and stir, being careful to avoid mixing the two layers entirely. Garnish with the candied ginger or lime wheel.

NOTES & VARIATIONS

This drink can also be served long in a Collins glass, if you prefer more kombucha. If flavored kombucha isn't available, plain will work just fine.

Other fruit juice and kombucha combinations to try:

· Black cherry juice, lemon juice, star-anise simple syrup, raspberry kombucha.

· Guava nectar, lime juice, makrut lime leaf simple syrup, berry kombucha.

2 oz [60 ml]
carrot juice

¾ oz [22 ml]
fresh lime juice

1 oz [30 ml]
orgeat (page 19) or
grenadine (page 19)

2 or 3 dashes
Angostura bitters
(optional)

Ginger-flavored
kombucha,
for topping

Candied ginger
or lime wheel,
for garnish

Just for the Hell of It

Five unorthodox spirits for cocktails

This book has covered a wide range of drinks and ingredients, and we hope you're on the path to finding that special fucking unicorn that speaks to your soul. Everyone's taste is unique, and that's for the better.

Like many cocktail books, we've focused our recipes around Western European and American spirits. Not only because they're more accessible for most readers, but also because that's where the roots of cocktail culture started. That isn't to say that liquors from other countries don't have a place in mixed drinks, just that they don't share the same history. Some have a strong tradition in their country of origin; others are traditionally served neat and are now finding a place in cocktails thanks to ever-inventive bartenders looking for something new.

This chapter is here to tickle your fancy and spark your imagination. Maybe you'll be compelled to try something off the beaten path next time you're out, or order something esoteric online. Keep exploring, and who knows what fucking magic you might stumble upon!

Sake & Soju

Sake 酒, Japanese rice wine (though more akin to beer in its brewing process), has a long tradition and nuanced culture in its homeland. In the West, sake is still shaking off the hangover of sake bombs and other mistreatments. Sake is more delicate and lower in alcohol (usually 18 to 20 percent ABV) than distilled liquors such as vodka and tequila and shouldn't be considered a direct substitute unless you're looking to lower the proof and change the character of your drink.

Soju 소주, is Korea's vodka and makes no apologies for what it is. It's a distilled liquor made from a variety of grains—often rice, wheat, or barley. Unlike vodka however, soju is most commonly sold pre-diluted to around 17 percent ABV.

So even though sake and pre-diluted soju are made quite differently, they have a similar strength and light flavor profile. Both function well in mixed drinks. Just save the good stuff for sipping neat.

Serving Suggestions

Sake
With its fruity and floral notes, sake makes an excellent replacement spirit in the **Bee's Knees** (page 37) or **Gin Fizz** (page 41). Why not throw a cheeky shot in your **Bellini** (page 50)?

Soju
Koreans love soju with lemon-lime soda, so why not try it in a **Pimm's Cup** (page 90) in place of the titular Pimm's? A spoon of Korean citron marmalade makes it even better. Or use soju in place of tequila in the **Watermelon Cooler** (page 84) for a lower-alcohol punch.

Baijiu

Relatively obscure in the West compared to its Japanese and Korean counterparts, baijiu 白酒 (pronounced *bye-joe* and literally translated as "white liquor") is a Chinese spirit distilled from one or more grains including sorghum, wheat, rice, and corn.

Unlike sake or soju, baijiu is usually high alcohol by volume and, compared to most Western clear spirits, super aggressive and pungent. This drink ain't no shy wallflower—it'll fucking cut a bitch! The distillation process is totally different from any other liquor, and it's the unique compounds that arise from that process that create its powerful funk.

Though traditionally served at mealtimes in shots, straight baijiu can be an *acquired* taste for the uninitiated. However, its varied range of styles and complex aromas make it an unorthodox and robust ingredient in cocktails for the daring. Just ensure your other ingredients have backbone. Adding baijiu to a Frozé (page 48) would be like adding a cruise missile to a ballet lesson!

Serving Suggestions

Ming River Sichuan Baijiu
A "strong aroma"-style baijiu specifically developed for the Western market with cocktails in mind. Try it in place of rum in a **Mai Tai** (page 58) but use 1 oz [30 ml] instead of 2 oz [60 ml]. Adding ⅔ oz [20 ml] to the **Kombucha Crackler** (page 109) will add a noticable kick to this fruity, funky beverage.

Kweichow Moutai Prince
A lighter "sauce aroma"-style baijiu from China's leading premium brand—has a powerful nose and notes of umami. Try it in place of blended Scotch in the **Penicillin** (page 75) but use 1 oz [30 ml] instead of 2 oz [60 ml]. The spice of the ginger and smoke of peat will be strong enough to balance the Chinese firewater. Or try 1 oz [30 ml] in place of vodka in a **Moscow Mule** (page 36).

Base Bitters

Enjoying the taste of bitterness has a learning curve. Nobody's born with a bitter-tooth. That said, ignoring what bitters can bring to a drink is like coloring without all the crayons. With thousands of chemical compounds that elicit the sensation of bitterness, it is by far the most complex of the five tastes.

Looking to start? A few dashes can make the difference between a good and a great cocktail. But just like a scene-stealing character actor, that bottle of Angostura bitters shouldn't be overlooked for a leading role!

Serving Suggestions

These drinks are extreme for some, so if you want to try at home, maybe start with fifty-fifty mix of bitters and pomegranate juice, or reduce the quantity by half. You've been warned!

Trinidad Especial

The first documented bitters-based cocktail. In an ice-filled cocktail shaker, combine 1 oz [30 ml] Angostura bitters, 1 oz [30 ml] oregeat, ⅔ oz [20 ml] fresh lime juice, and ⅓ oz [10 ml] pisco. Shake. Strain into a chilled coupe glass. *Origin:* Valentino Bolognese (2008).

Angostura Collins

A **Tom Collins** (page 41) but without the gin. In an ice-filled cocktail shaker combine 1 oz [30 ml] fresh lemon juice and 1 oz [30 ml] rich simple syrup. Shake well. Strain into an ice-filled Collins glass and float 1 oz [30 ml] Angostura bitters on top of the sour mix. Carefully top with soda water to keep the layers. Serve with a straw, unstirred so that the drinker can mix. *Origin:* Jamie Boudreau at Canon, Seattle (2011).

Fernet-Branca

Amari, bitter Italian liqueurs, are seeing a resurgence in cocktails. Even so, not every bottle can be as popular as the sunny, citrusy Campari and Aperol or approachable Averna. Yes, they're bitter, but they're really not so hard to like. Other bottles are more... niche in appeal.

Fernet is bitter and sweet, but even more bitter. Also medicinal and mentholated. It's a difficult drink, undeniably divisive, and bartenders love it. It's not for everyone and that's the point. And if it's not for you, don't feel bad about it.

But, for the irrepressibly curious, here's what they do with it. We'd advise you to try these drinks at a bar before you invest in your own bottle.

Serving Suggestions

Hanky Panky
A **Martini** (page 38) variation. In an ice-filled mixing glass, combine 1½ oz [45 ml] sweet vermouth, 1½ oz [45 ml] gin and 2 dashes of Fernet-Branca. Stir and strain into a chilled martini glass.

Toronto
An **Old Fashioned** (page 69) with the addition of ¼ oz [7.5 ml] Fernet-Branca. *Origin:* Revived by Jamie Boudreau at Canon, Seattle (2011).

Aquavit & Malört

Sweden's most famous liquor may be aquavit, a spice-infused vodka (typically with caraway or dill). It's most infamous cultural export might be Malört, the drink named for the Swedish word for "wormwood."

Jeppson's Malört is a Chicago institution/inside joke, kind of like the Cubs. In terms of mass appeal, it makes Fernet-Branca look like Coca-fucking-Cola.

Both liquors, along with vodka, come under the category of *brännvin*, which in Sweden is usually served as small shots (snaps) with meals and drinking songs.

Here's how you can put them into delicious cocktails, instead. Though, you should learn the songs. Life's too damn short to not learn a few drinking songs, even in Swedish. *Helan går!*

Serving Suggestions

Malmö Mule
A **Moscow Mule** (page 36) but replace the vodka with aquavit.

Bloody Max Martin
A **Bloody Mary** (page 60) but replace the vodka with aquavit.

The Hard Sell
A **Corpse Reviver No. 2** (page 66) variation. In an ice-filled cocktail shaker, combine ¾ oz [22 ml] gin, ¾ oz [22 ml] elderflower liqueur, ¾ oz [22 ml] Jeppson's Malört, ¾ oz [22 ml] fresh lemon juice, and 1 dash absinthe or anise liqueur. Shake. Strain into a chilled coupe glass and garnish with the expressed oil of a grapefruit peel. *Origin:* Brad Bolt at Bar DeVille, Chicago (2009).

Acknowledgments

This book could not have happened without the amazing team at Chronicle Books. Thank you to Alison Petersen, Michelle Clair, April Whitney, Natalie Nicolson, Olivia Roberts, and Maggie Edelman. And a particular, heartfelt, extra-fucking-special thanks to Kim Romero, my editor at Chronicle since 2012 and head cheerleader of the Calligraphuck line. Thanks to your hard work and advocacy over the years, this has grown from just a little Indiegogo project into more than I could have ever imagined.

To my friends and family for listening to me bitch and moan through the writing process— my brothers and mum and dad, Hannes, Dwane, Barry, Masud, and the crew at Angel Comedy Club. Thanks for the coffee and encouragement.

I owe a great debt to all the professional bartenders out there for creating such a flourishing culture for me to blatantly steal from, like the dirty artist I am.

A special thanks to Dave Arnold, firstly for his work at the cutting-edge of cocktail culture. But more importantly, it was through his *Cooking Issues* podcast that I first learned of the Museum of Food and Drink (MOFAD) in Brooklyn. Which is where I met my most valuable partner in this book, and in life, Melissa.

To my darling wife, thank you for being supportive in countless ways through this process. You keep proving every day that marrying you was the best decision of my life. I promise now that this thing is completed, I'll finally put up that fucking IKEA shelf like I promised.

Library of Congress Cataloging-in-Publication Data
Names: Calligraphuck Ltd., author. | Boman, Linus, author.
Title: Classy as fuck cocktails : 60 damn good recipes for all occasions / Calligraphuck ; [Linus Boman].
Description: San Francisco : Chronicle Books, 2020. | Authors name from publisher's galley. Introduction carries the signature, "Linus."
Identifiers: LCCN 2019057503 | ISBN 9781452182667 (hardback)
Subjects: LCSH: Cocktails. | LCGFT: Cookbooks.
Classification: LCC TX951 .C5293 2020 | DDC 641.87/4--dc23
LC record available at https://lccn.loc.gov/2019057503

ISBN: 978-1-4521-8266-7

Manufactured in China.

Design by Linus Boman.

10 9 8 7 6 5 4 3

Chronicle books and gifts are available at special quantity discounts to corporations, professional associations, literacy programs, and other organizations. For details and discount information, please contact our corporate/premiums department at corporatesales@chroniclebooks.com or at 1-800-759-0190.

Chronicle Books LLC
680 Second Street
San Francisco, California 94107
www.chroniclebooks.com

Index

About the Author

Linus Boman is a lettering artist, designer, and design communicator based in London. He is a former stand-up comic and a cofounder of Angel Comedy Club in Islington, London.

He's also the founder of Calligraphuck, the premier source for gifts and stationery products featuring exquisite expletives.

Linus is a passionate home bartender and makes pretty damn good Korean fried chicken. This book combines his love of libations, lettering, and four-letter words.

You can find his work here:
www.timesnewboman.com